Famous Explorers™

Jacques Cartier

Jeff
Donaldson-Forbes

The Rosen Publishing Group's
PowerKids Press™
New York

To Matthew Manning-Mithout

Published in 2002 by The Rosen Publishing Group, Inc.
29 East 21st Street, New York, NY 10010

First Edition

Book Design: Maria E. Melendez and Felicity Erwin
Project Editors: Kathy Campbell, Jennifer Landau, Jennifer Quasha

Photo Credits: Cover and title page, pp. 6, 8, 10, 14, 15 (right), 16 (background) © North Wind Picture Archives; p. 4 © Bettmann/CORBIS; p. 5 © Dave G. Houser/CORBIS; pp. 7, 12, 15 (left), 16, 17, 19 © The Granger Collection, New York; pp. 7, 11 © CORBIS; p. 8 (great auk) © Academy of Natural Sciences/CORBIS; p. 19 (inset) © Gianni Dagli Orti/CORBIS; p. 16 (Map of Cartier's expeditions) illustrated by Maria E. Melendez.

Donaldson-Forbes, Jeff.
Jacques Cartier / Jeff Donaldson-Forbes—1st ed.
   p. cm.— (Famous explorers)
ISBN 0-8239-5834-5
1. Cartier, Jacques, 1491–1557—Juvenile literature. 2. Explorers—America—Biography—Juvenile literature. 3. Explorers—France—Biography—Juvenile literature. 4. America—Discovery and exploration—French—Juvenile literature. 5. Canada—Discovery and exploration—French—Juvenile literature. 6. Canada—History—To 1763 (New France)—Juvenile literature. [1. Cartier, Jacques 1491–1557. 2. Explorers. 3. Canada—Discovery and exploration—French.] I. Title. II. Series.
   E133.C3 D66 2002
   971'.01'13'092—dc21

                                                                                    00–012391

Contents

A World of Discovery

Jacques Cartier was born in 1491 in Saint-Malo, a fishing town in northern France. During Cartier's youth, many European explorers were searching for the **Northwest Passage** to Asia. The explorers believed that by sailing west they eventually would reach China or India. European merchants hoped to buy silk fabrics and gold and silver treasures in these countries. In 1497, the explorer John Cabot sailed from England in search of the Northwest Passage. After his return, Cabot told stories of the many fish that swam near a place he called Newfoundland. The fishermen in Saint-Malo were excited to learn about new places to fish. Fishermen in Saint-Malo began sailing to Newfoundland when Cartier was a young man. It is likely that Cartier traveled on some of these fishing **expeditions**.

In this picture of Jacques Cartier, he is shown standing in front of a map of Canada and Newfoundland. Right: This statue honors John Cabot, who discovered Newfoundland.

5

An Experienced Sailor

While sailing with the fishermen of Saint-Malo, Cartier became interested in **navigation**. He learned to use star charts and other tools that allowed him to know where his ship was in the sea. Cartier became a great navigator. Some historians believe that Cartier sailed on a voyage to Brazil as a young man. Others think he traveled with Giovanni da Verrazano, who sailed along the eastern coast of North America in 1524. Though we aren't certain of Cartier's actual early journeys, we know that he became an experienced sailor. King Francis I, the king of France, heard about Cartier's experience as a navigator. In 1534, the king wanted to send an expedition to search for the Northwest Passage.

Above: Giovanni da Verrazano sailed along the eastern coast of North America in 1524. Right: This painting of King Francis I is by Jean Clouet. Left: Explorer Samuel de Champlain made this map of the northeast coast of North America in 1607.

He hoped that the expedition would find new lands and bring back treasures from the New World. He chose Jacques Cartier to lead the expedition. Cartier kept detailed **journals** of his travels that have allowed historians to trace his journey.

Pais de rochers & desert,
Bons parts.

C. des Chateaux

Carpunc
I. aux oiseaux

C. double

C. Raze

da

Pointu

TER
RE
NEV
VE

C. de Bonne
Veuë

R. Roye

C. de
Lorraine

C. de Raze

C. S. Marie

I. S. Pierre

Le grand Bans aux Morues

The Strait of Belle Isle

On April 20, 1534, Cartier's expedition sailed from Saint-Malo. On May 10, the expedition reached Cape Bonavista on the eastern coast of Newfoundland. Cartier and his men needed food. They traveled to a nearby island called the Isle of Birds, today called Funk Island. Thousands of **great auks** lived on the island. Great auks were birds that could not fly and were easy for Cartier's men to catch. They killed enough great auks to keep themselves fed for the rest of the voyage. The expedition then sailed northwest to the Bay of Castles, where bad weather forced them to stop for two weeks. On June 9, Cartier discovered that there was a **strait** of water that ran south from the Bay of Castles. He named it the Strait of Belle Isle.

Top: *This painting of great auks is by John James Audubon.*
Bottom: *This map of Newfoundland is from 1609.*

Newfoundland and Canada

This picture shows islands at the opening of the Saint Lawrence River.

Farther south, the Strait of Belle Isle opened into a larger body of water. Today that water is known as the Gulf of Saint Lawrence. On June 15, 1534, the expedition sailed to the western coast of Newfoundland. Cartier mapped the rocky and dangerous coast as he traveled south. Cartier could see that it would not be an easy place for French **settlers** to live. Before reaching the end of the Newfoundland coast, Cartier continued looking for the Northwest Passage to Asia. The expedition reached many sites in what is now known as the Canadian **province** of New Brunswick. On June 30, they reached Prince Edward Island. The island was covered with trees and fruit bushes. It was very different from the rocky coast of Newfoundland.

The expedition sailed even farther west and on July 3 reached another large body of water. Cartier at first believed this might be the entrance to the Northwest Passage, but he soon realized it was only a bay. He named it the Bay of Chaleur.

On July 3, 1534, Cartier reached a body of water he named the Bay of Chaleur.

Meeting the Micmacs

On July 6, while exploring the Bay of Chaleur, Cartier's men saw about 50 canoes sailing toward them. The canoes were carrying a group of Native Americans. Cartier did not know if the Native Americans were friendly. He had the cannons on his ships fire a warning, but the Native Americans continued to approach. They used sign language to show that they were friendly. Cartier learned that the Native Americans called themselves the Micmacs. The Micmacs traded with the Frenchmen, exchanging furs and meat for small knives and glass beads. Cartier was disappointed that the Micmacs did not have any gold or silver, but the meeting was still useful. Cartier began to learn the Micmac language that would allow him to communicate with other Native Americans on his trip.

Top: *Native Americans traded with beads like those shown here.*
Bottom: *This picture shows Iroquois, the Native American group that Cartier met after the Micmacs, building a birchbark canoe.*

Ruler of the Iroquois

The expedition sailed north from the Bay of Chaleur along the Gaspé **Peninsula**. Bad weather forced the men to go ashore. They encountered a group of about 300 Native Americans who were fishing there. These were the Iroquois

Donnaconna, the Iroquois leader, is shown approaching Cartier's ship.

people. This first encounter was friendly. However, on July 24, Cartier did something that made the Iroquois ruler, Donnaconna, very angry. Cartier wanted to claim the land for France. He raised a large wooden cross with a sign that read, "Long Live the King of France." Though he did not understand the French language, Donnaconna knew what Cartier was doing and became upset. Cartier gave Donnaconna gifts to make peace. Donnaconna agreed to let

Taignoagny and Domagaya, his two sons, travel with Cartier. Cartier wanted to teach the boys to speak French and to use them as guides on future expeditions. The expedition headed home to France, reaching Saint-Malo on September 5, 1534.

This is a picture of an Iroquois warrior.

When Cartier claimed the Gaspé Peninsula for France, he made Donnaconna angry.

15

JACQUES CARTIER'S
Routes
(1534)
(1535) – (1536)

HUDSON
BAY

Strait of
Belle Isle

Funk Island

Cape
Bonavista

NEWFOUNDLAND

Cape Race

NEW FRANCE
(CANADA)

ONTARIO

Saint Lawrence River

Gulf of
Saint Lawrence

Bay of
Chaleur

Cape
Breton
Island

Lake Superior

Stadacona (Quebec)

Hochelaga (Montreal)
October 1535

Prince
Edward
Island

Port Royal

Lake Huron

NOVA SCOTIA

Lake Michigan

Toronto

Lake Ontario

ATLANTIC
OCEAN

Lake Erie

A Second Expedition

King Francis I was pleased with Cartier's expedition. Though Cartier had not discovered the Northwest Passage, King Francis believed that there were great treasures to be found in the New World. On October 30, 1534, King Francis I authorized Cartier to lead a second expedition even larger than the first. Cartier commanded a crew of 110 men, an enormous ship named the *Great Ermine*, and two smaller ships called the *Small Ermine* and the *Sparrowhawk*. Taignoagny and Domagaya, the sons of the Iroquois ruler Donnaconna, had learned to speak French and would travel with Cartier. On May 19, 1535, Cartier's second expedition sailed from Saint-Malo.

Above: *King Francis I, shown here, let Cartier lead a second expedition.* Top: *This map shows the routes of Cartier's 1534 and 1535 expeditions.* Middle: *Cartier speaks with an Iroquois in 1535.* Bottom: *This is a picture of Cartier's ships leaving Saint-Malo.*

Saguenay and Canada

On June 25, the expedition was hit by a storm that lasted for weeks. The three ships were separated from each other, and they did not meet again for more than a month. On July 26, all three ships arrived at the western end of the Strait of Belle Isle. On September 1, following directions given to him by Taignoagny and Domagaya, Cartier led the expedition into the Saint Lawrence River. Taignoagny and Domagaya explained that by traveling down the river, Cartier would reach the country of the Iroquois people, called Saguenay. Beyond Saguenay lay more land called Canada. When the expedition reached Saguenay, Taignoagny and Domagaya called out to a group of Iroquois people on land. The Iroquois were excited to learn that Donnaconna's sons

Top: This Iroquois warrior holds an axelike weapon called a tomahawk.
Bottom: This is a printed plan of the Iroquois village of Hochelaga.

had come home. The expedition went ashore and followed the Iroquois to the village of Stadacona, near the site of today's Quebec. In Stadacona the boys were reunited with their father, Donnaconna.

LA TERRA DE HOCHELAGA
NELLA NOVA FRANCIA.

MONTE REAL.

La Chine

Cartier left the larger ships anchored in the water near Stadacona. He took a small crew with him to continue exploring the Saint Lawrence River. On October 2, 1535, Cartier and his men reached the Native American village of Hochelaga. Near Hochelaga, Cartier climbed a large hill and could see giant waterfalls farther down the Saint Lawrence River. The waterfalls made it impossible for the crew to continue. Cartier still believed that he might be near China, and he named the waterfalls "La Chine." Cartier knew that it was too late in the season to sail home to France. He and his crew returned to Stadacona to camp for the winter. The winter was very hard for the French. Many men fell ill and died. When it was time to sail home, there were not enough men to operate all three ships so the *Small Ermine* was left behind.

Cartier named the waterfalls he found "La Chine," thinking he was near China.

The Failed Fort

The expedition reached Saint-Malo on July 16, 1536. In 1541, Cartier traveled to Canada with French settlers and built a fort near Stadacona, called Charlesbourg Royal. The Iroquois did not welcome the settlers at Charlesbourg Royal and attacked the French fort. The Iroquois attacks forced the settlers to return to France with Cartier in 1542. Cartier never returned to Canada, but his explorations allowed the French to continue settling new lands. His maps and journals provided valuable information for other explorers in the years to come. Jaques Cartier died in Saint-Malo on September 1, 1557.

Cartier's Timeline

1491 Jacques Cartier is born in Saint-Malo, France.

1534 On June 9, Cartier discovers the Strait of Belle Isle.

1535 On October 2, Cartier reaches the village of Hochelaga.

1541 Cartier leads an expedition to found a fort in Stadacona.

1557 Cartier dies in Saint-Malo, France.

Glossary

expeditions (ek-spuh-DIH-shunz) Trips for a special purpose such as scientific study.

great auks (GRAYT AWKS) Birds that couldn't fly which were hunted by humans until they became extinct around 1850.

journals (JER-nuhlz) Notebooks in which people write their thoughts.

navigation (nah-vuh-GAY-shun) A way of figuring out which way a ship is headed.

Northwest Passage (NORTH-west PAS-idge) A passage explorers believed eventually would reach China or India.

peninsula (peh-NIN-suh-luh) A piece of land that sticks into water from a larger body of land.

province (PRAH-vehns) A section of a larger country, like a state.

settlers (SEH-tuh-lerz) People who move to a new land to live.

strait (STRAYT) A narrow passage that connects two bodies of water.

Index

Web Sites

Due to the changing nature of Internet links, PowerKids Press has developed an online list of Web sites related to the subject of this book. This site is updated regularly. Please use this link to access the list: www.powerkidslinks.com/famex/carti/

DATE			